THE FIELD WORKER

Short Stories and Learnings

RENANTE SALCEDO

To the communities I work with,

To my friends and colleagues who share my passion,

To my family who supports me all the way,

To God who gives me strength and guidance.

CONTENTS

ACKNOWLEDGMENT

To the people who helped make this book possible,

my sincere thanks.

PREFACE

When I was still a kid, I dreamt of publishing my own comic book. I was very much amazed by comic books. They were very illustrative, entertaining and even educating.

With scrap papers and pencil, I imagine stories and used to make comic strips of it.

I kept dreaming, drawing, making my own comic strips –on scrap papers.

That dream came true.

But that dream's reality only happened decades later, when I started working -- working with the communities -- as a field worker.

My first published comic magazine was an advocacy material on fishery management for the fishing communities back in 1998. Then, in later years, comic strips on various advocacy themes were again published in informational magazines supported by non-government organizations I worked with.

Yes, I work with non-government organizations -in my entire work life. This allowed me to engage with various communities, whether upland, coastal, rural and urban poor.

This is my passion. A passion that grew inside me when I was still in my college days. The days when I also discovered my love for writing.

I spent around twenty years working with communities. I learned many things from them. I learned from the community people I worked with. I learned from my colleagues. I also learned from me – from the things I did and from my mistakes.

I learned values and virtues that helped me through life and through working with communities.

Last Christmas, after 20 years from my first published comic magazine, I was staring at the heaven asking, "God, what do you want me to do next?"

So, this book.

This book aims to share those learnings to you. The stories in this book are based on real events– the experiences from the field. This book is for everyone who works or goes to the communities-- whether full time, part time or just a visit.

This is for you.

THE AUTHOR
April 2019

INTRODUCTION

S he came into the office with a frowning face. Disappointed. She just arrived the night before from a distant tribal village for a 2-day community training. Last week, she was very busy preparing for that event. She was very excited.

But this morning, she came in disappointed. The training did not happen. The tribal folks who were supposed to attend that training were not there.

What happened?

I learned that the tribal council did not knew well about the activity. Their consent was not sought.

This is not supposed to happen.

But, many of us who work in the field, at some point, at some time, encounter this, or something like this, or maybe worse than this.

We feel disappointed, discouraged, annoyed, demoralized or even enraged.

Our expectations are not met.

We planned for weeks. We have prepared everything with a high expectation of an event to perfectly happen.

But then –it did not happen –as perfectly expected.

Then, we blame. We blame not ourselves, but the community or our colleagues for not helping.

Something is not right. Something is missing in the preparation.

What is missing?

We miss to consider the side of the community. We miss the value of understanding the communities. We miss to prepare the very essential values within ourselves in working with the communities – as field worker.

In my twenty years of working in the field, in various communities, I learned the values of working with them.

This book will share that to you.

The Field Worker, is a collection of short stories based from real experiences I encountered in the field, read Part II. These are short stories of engaging with the farmers, the urban poor, the fisherfolk, the indigenous peoples and women.

Before that, I also wanted to share how I came to love working at the field -- with the communities. In Part I are stories of events that, I say, influenced me and how my passion grew as a field worker.

In Part III, this book shares the learnings I had in working with the communities. These learnings are values and virtues all field workers –whether full time or part time – must inculcate in his or her mind, heart and soul.

Without these values, field work to the communities, may have no good results. The learnings shared in this book will contribute to being better and effective in field work –in working with communities.

But these stories and learnings are not just for community organizers or community development facilitators or for those who work in non-government organizations whose main services are for the communities.

Learnings in this book can also be taken by those whose works or interests involve fields, communities and people, in whatever degree -- whether one is a doctor who goes to the village, an engineer who builds roads in rural areas, a sales agent who delivers goods to far-flung towns, an entrepreneur who wants to invest in farms, a forester, a student intern who is doing field studies, a field researcher, a sociology teacher, a geologist, a social worker, a church worker, an environment advocate, a mountaineer who goes to forest villages or a tourist who travels to places of various cultures.

It will help you in dealing with various types of people, in one way or another, especially, in dealing with the rural folks.

PART I.
PRELUDE TO
FIELDWORK

THE SCRAP PAPERS

T hose were precious to me – scrap papers, in those years, when I was still a kid. My father used to bring some from his work --used papers meant to be in the garbage. I kept them.

I made sketches on those scrap papers with a pencil. I drew comic superheroes. I drew Superman, Batman, Spiderman, Incredible Hulk. I drew robots too, like, Voltes 5, Mazinger Z and Transformers.

I also used to buy comic magazines. With my small school allowance that time, I saved some for months until I can buy comic magazines. I usually bought the old ones which were cheaper.

Amazed by the illustrations and stories, I thought of making my own. So, with the scrap papers, I made stories and illustrated them as comic strips.

That became a dream. I thought, one day I can

publish a comic book. A desire I kept for years to come true.

In my college days, those experiences in sketching comic strips in scrap papers found its way into the student publication. I became the publication cartoonist. I had my sketches and illustrations printed in that student publication.

After college, my experience in the student publication as cartoonist led to the publication of the first comic magazine I created –- an environmental advocacy comic published by a non-government organization I worked with.

THE MOUNTAINEER-ING SOCIETY

My first taste of remote villages was when we organized the mountaineering society in our school.

It was for fun first, for adventure.

The group trekked at remote villages at country sides, crossed rivers and climbed mountains. We did it on holidays and summer.

Trips and treks to places were organized. More and more students got attracted and joined.

But, the more we trek, the more students joining, the more we need to learn and be responsible.

First, we tapped a doctor to discuss about first aid in cases of injuries during trips. At one instance, the group coordinated with mountain fire brigade for an orientation of what to do in case we encounter forest and grass fires.

Then, we tapped environmental advocates for an orientation on forest conservation and the do's and don'ts when we are inside the forest.

Some of us then went into learning some more, such as, understanding the indigenous peoples who live in the forest.

For me, it was not only appreciating the natural beauty of mountains, rivers and forests then, but, I started to appreciate people and culture.

This led me to my interest with engaging the remote villages.

THE PORTABLE TYPEWRITER

I was very happy when my parents bought a portable typewriter. In those days it was like a laptop.

Before that, I wrote articles for the student publication using my handwriting—with a pen in yellow pad papers.

Yes, I learned to write. I discovered it later in my mid college days.

How did I knew about writing?

I remember my English teacher then asked our class one time to write an essay on what are we if we are an animal. I wrote about being a bird and explained it. After reading my essay, my teacher told me I have the potential to write.

That then pushed me to contribute to the student publication. So, I just don't do cartoons, I also wrote articles for that publication.

That portable typewriter was some kind of a high technology already at that time. Again, it is like a laptop today I can carry to places.

So, I wrote a lot. I wrote stories and articles for the publications, I also wrote poems –with that portable typewriter.

My engagement with the student publication has opened many more learnings and discoveries.

With my co-student writers, we learned more about campus paper management, magazine lay-out, photography, editorial cartooning, news and feature writing, with other writers from other schools in the country.

We shared experiences.

The best thing I learned was on the purpose of writing– on what to write – that our task was to inform, educate and mobilize.

I was exposed to realities beyond the walls of the

Renante Salcedo

classrooms and the gates of schools. I was exposed to the rural and urban poor communities.

From there, I started to write about what was happening in the society -- about students' welfare, the farmers' plight, the indigenous peoples' cause and the workers' rights.

With this, my passion for social change grew.

PART II. SHORT STORIES FROM THE FIELD

DREAMS IN BALLOT BOXES

Bukidnon Province, 1999

It was early morning when we secretly transported the ballot boxes in an *Elf* truck.

"It's going to be a tough ride!" my colleague who drove the truck told us.

Going to the remote farming village through the dirt roads, we always got stuck in the wet and muddy parts caused by the other night's heavy rain.

"We're again stuck in the mud! Please push." my colleague said again.

We all got down from the truck and pushed, around 5 of us. Our feet got muddy. Each time we were stuck, we have to get down and push. Then climbed up the truck again.

But we need to be fast. We need to hurry. We don't

want others to notice.

I felt danger and excitement. This is the day! This is it!

But then, the *Elf* truck was stuck again in deep mud. Our human power to push was not enough. Then a farmer with a carabao passed by.

"Sir, can we ask help? Can you pull the truck with your carabao? We are stuck." Another colleague asked the farmer.

He agreed. We tied a rope to the truck. Then, the carabao pulled. The tires slowly got out from the mud. It was successful! The truck got out.

We climbed back up again. We rode the next hour going to that remote farming village where the farmers were waiting.

As we approached, I saw their faces of mixed reactions.

"Here we are! We have what you have been waiting for!" I told the group happily.

For almost a year, we have been assisting this

farming village of their quest. Now, this is the day. The quest is fulfilled. This is the day that this remote farming village dreamt of for decades. A dream that they believe for years will just remain a dream. The dream for land they till as their own.

The ballot boxes were filled with land titles for these farmers. It was transported secretly to avoid the noses of bandits, opportunists and landlord goons who doesn't want the land to be distributed to this farming village.

The quest for land to own by farmers is never easy, even with the passing of the land reform law. In this part of the country, it has been bloody. Several groups came here for land. One group quarrels with another.

This is the day! As the land titles were distributed to the farmers, festivity was on the air. We dance and sung. Happiness filled the atmosphere.

THOUGHT-PROVOKING MACHINE

Agusan del Sur, 2013

I was still sleepy. I had to wake up early for a travel. I was fetched by the company's pick-up vehicle. It was still dark as we left the house to visit that far-flung rice farming community in another region.

Rock 'n roll, slow rock and love songs were played by the driver as we zoom the national highway at a speed of 100 kph for almost 5 hours.

We sang with the music and laughed as a colleague broke jokes. It was a happy long trip. We stopped for breakfast along the way.

In my mind, we have to reach that community before noon. We are inspecting something. We need to know if that thing works. I was excited. Then, visit another community.

We were greeted with a smile by the farmer who received us.

"We had it!" He said referring to the machine.

We were all happy then. At last, it arrived. They were waiting for this for some years now. A machine that will help them in rice farming – a combine harvester. It is a machine that reaps, threshes and winnows rice grains ready for sacking as it passes –– in one process.

Very efficient and advance machine.

We saw the machine. It's now owned by that far-flung rice farming community. A government grant to them in support to land reform and rural development.

We were there to monitor.

The farmer, who was also chosen to operate the machine, demonstrated to us how the machine works.

But as we discussed its effectivity, a little sorrow got into his eyes. Something that was not good despite the machine's effectivity.

He asked, "With this machine that only needs three persons to operate, what happened to the many farm laborers?"

"What do you mean?" I wondered.

"The farm laborers here traditionally work together to do the harvesting, the threshing and rice sacking. They will be replaced with this machine. What will be their income for their families?" Is there alternative livelihood for them?" He continued asking.

I paused. It was thought-provoking. It was saddening. I have no answer at that time. I agreed with the farmer on that concern.

"Ummm...I'll include your apprehension in the monitoring report." I just then told him.

After around 2 hours of checking other things, we went back to our pick-up vehicle to go to another town. It will be again another 2-3 hours travel.

But this time, we travelled silently.

My mind kept remembering his questions. It really struck me deeply. The vision of a farming community to have access to land, services and farm facilities is something to think about.

"Are we really doing the right thing? Will that

machine really economically help the farming community?" I kept asking myself.

We need to look at rural development deeper.

OUT IN THE DARK AND COLD

Macajalar Bay, 1998

It was dark, cold and quiet night. The lights I saw were glitters from the coastlines and from the lamps coming from other fishing boats. We were there for hours in small fishing boats in the middle of the sea.

We were not there to fish, we were looking for something.

We had radios and flashlights with us. I had a camera, a pen, papers and other documents wrapped in plastic bag so not to get wet. My other colleague in another boat had a compass and a map.

In that morning, we still had a training at the fisherfolk center in the shoreline. Then, a meeting in the afternoon. As the night fell, we took our dinner, changed our clothes, we put on our jackets and life vests. The fisherfolk checked their boats. They filled the boat engines with gasoline and prepared extra liters in containers. They also filled the *lamparas* with kerosene.

We prepared three boats. I boarded in one of them with other fisherfolk.

We waited for the waves to mellow down before we pushed the boats to the sea.

I had mixed emotion. I knew it's dangerous. But I felt the urge to do what we had planned to do.

We had been crossing the sea for some hours already. The fisherfolk leader radioed the other boats if they saw something. Nothing yet.

As we moved to another part of the sea, the other boats radioed us. "We got it! We had a sighting!"

"Let's wait first! Let's not move yet. Put out your lights, we don't want them to notice!" The leader from another boat screamed in the radio.

We waited for some time. Patiently.

It's dark, cold and quiet. We were getting ready. My heart pumped faster as I sat tightly in that fishing boat.

Then, a radio signal came. We moved fast!

"You are under arrest!" The fisherman shouted as we approached a big fishing vessel that illegally fished inside regulated waters. The big fishing net was already submerged in the sea that the big fishing vessel cannot escape easily.

It was a success! We boarded the fishing vessel, a colleague read the boat captain of his rights and did some documentation.

For years, these fisherfolk complained about these big fishing vessels owned by influential millionaire businessmen who fish near shorelines. The law prohibit such. With advanced fishing technology and large nets, these big fishing vessels can catch hundreds of tons of fishes leaving the small fisherfolk with nothing more to catch.

With the government's fishery bureau, these fisherfolk were trained on fishery laws and were deputized as fishery wardens so they can apprehend illegal fishers. We were there to organize and help strengthen the group.

While still with no proper sleep, we went to another fishing village in the next morning. Now, we brought the prepared visual aids in manila papers for the mangrove planting training.

Tired but fulfilled.

THROUGH THE
SWAMPS

Butuan Bay, 2004

The sun was just rising. The fisherfolk group started preparing many things –kitchen utensils, firewood, big cooking wares and drinking water in large containers. A live pig was also tied tightly.

I was also checking my personal stuff while waiting for them -- my extra shirts, shorts, a cap, a pen and a note book.

Four dugout canoes were prepared. A dugout canoe is a boat made of a half of a tree trunk – a log-- where the center is hollowed to make space for persons.

"How long is the trip?" I asked the fisherfolk leader.

"Maybe an hour ride with these canoes." He answered.

Whew! Aboard a canoe with no outrigger for an hour ride. I was thinking this was an adventure.

Everyone seemed happy. They were waiting for this day. A woman fisherfolk kept singing. I forgot her song but not the melody.

I have been with them for some three years already. I can still remember the first time we met—during a participatory resource assessment where we evaluated the status of their coastal resources, fishing gears commonly used, fish species they usually catch and their volume of catch over the years.

We found out in that assessment that their fish catch was declining and that the fish habitats were gradually damaged. They kept recalling that fish catch were better before. They wanted to rehabilitate the costal resources. They also wanted to have other sources of income aside from capture fishing.

We had several training and planning sessions to organize and strengthen their group. The other year, they were very active in the coastal resource rehabilitation. They planted mangroves with other fisherfolk groups we organized.

"Are we all ready to go?" The leader asked the group.

They answered yes.

We then one-by-one stepped on the canoe. Slowly. Balancing.

It's my time to board. I was quite nervous. I had to make a good balance so the canoe won't flip down.

"Just relax, don't get nervous. Just stay in the middle and go with the flow." The fisherman instructed me how to ride the canoe, smiling.

Around 4 of us were in one canoe. The rest of the canoes have around 3 to 4 people aboard.

Then, the fishermen started paddling. Slowly, we moved.

We passed by narrow but deep creeks.

Now I understood why we used the dugout canoes, boats with outriggers cannot pass into these narrow creeks.

My nervousness subsided after some minutes. I kept thinking – stay still and just go with the flow.

Just sit in the middle and have balance.

As we trekked the creeks, we were passing through lots of mangroves, *nipas* and other kinds of swamp trees. I saw several fishes below. I imagined, we were like inside a maze of several creeks in a swampland.

But, the fisherfolk knew where to go.

"Are there crocodiles here?" I asked.

"Yes. But they are less seen nowadays. Are you afraid?" One of the fisherfolk answered laughing.

"Yes! Of course!" I replied.

They all laughed and said not to worry.

After an hour, we reached the place, a creek-side land surrounded by mangrove trees, *nipa* and tall grasses.

One by one we got off the canoes. We also disembarked all the things we brought.

We made it.

Now, they prepared the cooking wares. They made a fire using the firewood we brought. Another group prepared the pig.

I understood that the pig we brought was not just for our food. It was also for the blessing ceremony -- for the start of their fishpond project.

The fisherfolk leader said "This is what we have been waiting for! We pray to God for the blessings that our efforts will be graced with abundance."

I sat at a big stone documenting quietly while they continued cleaning the pig. They cut its meat. Some parts were cooked in boiling water without salt. The rest of the meat were cooked for our foods.

Then, we all ate and celebrated.

They have been preparing this fishpond for weeks. Today was a blessing time. In few days from now, they will already put the *tilapia* fingerlings they accessed from the government fishery bureau.

They hoped for this long before – another source of income, an aquaculture project, an alternative to capture fishing.

BREAKING THE
DISCOMFORT

Mt Malindang, 1999

W e were both sitting on the ground near his farm.

I had travelled here from the mountain town center by foot and horse ride for almost 3 hours to meet him -- the tribe elder.

I was uncomfortable yet as there was silence. I can hear my guide talking to him a while ago in their local dialect before he approached me. I cannot understand them.

We both sat on the ground. Quietly—for some minutes. He was just looking at me. A farm bolo was tucked in his waist.

We were like both waiting to break the silence— who will talk first.

It's our first time to meet each other.

I reached inside my backpack a pack of cigarette. I lit a stick. After some puff, I offered to him the pack.

He got one and lit the cigarette with his match.

He smiled.

I smiled too.

"Would it be fine to ask you some questions?" I asked him in my own local dialect.

"Yes!" he answered smiling using my dialect.

"Do you know why I am here?" I asked again.

"Yes, she told me your intention." He answered referring to my local guide who talked to him a while ago.

So, I got my questionnaire tool and pen and started asking the questions. I wrote the answers in the questionnaire.

"How far is the source of your water for drinking?" I asked one of the questions.

He looked up the sky and was silent for a while before he answered, "...ahhh, I leave home when the sun is just rising. The sun is already that high when I come back home after fetching water."

This time I have to estimate the distance based on his sun observation and walking speed, "That's a bit far." I said.

"Maybe, that is the nearest source." he replied.

"So, what are you planting now?" I asked him.

"I'm preparing to plant onions and root crops." He answered.

"Are those for sale? The crops you are planting?" I

asked him again.

"The onions? Yes. The root crops are just for our consumption." He replied.

I checked the boxes in the questionnaire for his answers.

"What a relief!" I said to myself silently with gladness as I almost finished the questions.

After some 30 minutes, we were finished.

Then the guide signaled to us, she looked at her watch and looked at the gloomy skies.

It's time for us to go.

"Do you want another one?" I again offered to him the cigarette pack as I lit another one. He got one.

We both got up. Stretched our arms. I offered a handshake to him and said sincerely. "Thank you for your time... it's an honor to meet. I still have to go to the next village."

He smiled while puffing the cigarette and answered, "May God bless your journey!"

Two weeks ago, I was one of the participants trained to conduct a rapid rural appraisal. We were oriented on the survey questionnaire, taught on how to asked questions and approximate some answers. We were going to do a survey at tribal communities in that far-flung mountain. The survey result was for a full blown project intervention for those upland communities in that mountain town.

A RIDE HOME

Mt Kalatungan, 2011

It was already late night when I reached my home in the city.

That was a trip!

I recalled earlier in the morning I was still in the mountain village some 1,400 meters above the sea.

I went to the tribal chieftain's house that morning to confirm our ride to the city. He was going to the city too.

I already packed my bag. I was there for almost a week already. I had several consultation meetings with the tribal elders, the local officials and church leaders to plan for a project entry. Some meetings during the day, some were in the evening.

So I waited for him – for his signal that we will ride.

"Datu, what vehicle are we hitching?" I asked

him.

He pointed at the vegetable truck.

The truck was still being filled with sacks and sacks of carrots. It was harvest time. The carrots will be delivered to the market in the city. From there, it will be transported to other cities in the north.

Aside from us, other villagers will also be hitching a ride to the city. There are no public transport going to and from that village – except for *habal-habal*, a passenger motorcycle.

We waited for all the sacks of carrots to be placed in the truck parked along rugged road.

It was almost lunch time when the driver signaled that we can climb the truck filled with sacks of carrots.

We climbed up the truck.

Good thing I already took my lunch early. It's going to be a long ride. There might be no chance I could eat at *carenderias* along the way.

"Just find a spot where you can place your feet." The chieftain told me. "This is usually how we go to the city. There are no four-wheeled passenger vehicle that go straight up here."

"I was told that riding *habal-habal* from here to the town center costs a thousand pesos!" I said.

"Yes, that's why it is common for us to hitch trucks. It is also free." the chieftain replied.

We were actually on top of the sacks of vegetables. Other hitchers have their spots and good grips on the sides of the truck and on the vegetable sacks.

"This is dangerous." I silently told myself.

Then, the engine started and the vegetable truck slowly moved. It cannot go fast because of the weight and the very rugged road.

We again passed by another village. I saw a pile of sacks of carrots and farmers waiting.

The truck stopped and we climbed down from it. The sacks of carrots were then piled in the truck. It is now very full with sacks of carrots.

"What time do you think we will reach the city?" I asked.

"Maybe, by late afternoon, if everything is fine." The chieftain replied.

Again, we all climbed up the truck. The truck moved again, slowly.

The road was really rough. Moving down, I saw the curve road ahead and a bridge. I saw the forest lines afar and a tapestry of farms at the sides.

Like the rest of the hitchers, I was bracing myself above the sacks of carrots, gripping the sacks for balance as the truck rolled over rugged and curvy roads.

We passed by the bridge. Slowly.

This went for hours. We were still midway to the city.

Then, we stopped.

"We had a flat tire!" the driver's assistant shouted.

"Uhhh...what?!" I told myself. "..in the middle of nowhere!"

The driver got out of his seat and checked the rear

tires. One of the rear tires exploded.

"We can still move, there's a tire shop ahead. Let's fix that there." The driver told his assistant.

"We might have ran into something sharp along the way. I checked the tires before we go." The assistant murmured.

Again, the truck moved.

It's getting dark as we reached the said tire shop in another village. They removed the flat tire and had the interior out and fixed.

We waited there for a while. It's quiet. I saw no people roaming. The few houses around already closed their windows and lights. The mountain breeze was getting colder. I got my jacket zipped and put the hood on.

"Are you hungry already?" I asked the chieftain.

"Yes, but I can still endure." He said smiling.

I pulled 2 packs of biscuits in my bag and offered one to him. We ate while waiting.

After an hour, the interior was fixed, put back inside the tire and re-installed.

Again, we moved. Slowly still. I observed we encountered only very few vehicles, most were vegetable trucks.

At last, we reached the concrete road. We were now at the town center. But, the city was still another 30 kilometers away.

We stopped a while near a closed store. I saw the driver got down, stretched his arms and then lit a cigarette.

"It is seven thirty." I said as I looked at the clock in my mobile phone. I saw other hitchers yawning already. They were sleepy and maybe hungry like us.

"Yeah..." the chieftain replied, "this is part of our life, we hitch trucks in going down towns and going up back to our villages. It is dangerous. Things happen along the way. But, this is our way of life."

The truck moved again. Now, it is a bit faster roving the cemented road.

As we approached the city, we were welcomed by glimmering lights from a distant—coming from subdivisions, commercial buildings and vehicles.

This time, we encountered many vehicles –cars, pick-ups, *jeepneys*, taxis and cargo trucks. Traffic was getting heavy.

At the street corners, I saw people walking, many are waiting for *jeepneys* and taxis and vendors selling in the sidewalk.

Stores and bars were still open. I heard music from a karaoke bar we just passed by.

The city was still very much alive.

We stopped twice at traffic lights until we reached the market.

"We are here!" the chieftain said.

"At last! What a trip!" I replied to him smiling as I climbed down and stretched my body.

"See you next week up there?" The chieftain asked.

"Yes, datu. See you next week. Thanks a lot!" I replied.

As we part ways, I then hailed a taxi for a ride home.

TREKKING THE MOUNTAIN

Mt Malindang, 1999

I t's raining hard that afternoon. I was in my rented room in a remote mountain town. I had my analogue mobile phone with an antenna, my notebook and some books I brought to read.

"What will I do? I was supposed to travel now." Thinking of my tasks. But I cannot go yet.

I phoned a friend in the city. Good thing that the phone signal is fine. We talked about anything -- about the weather, latest news I haven't heard and about work. We talked for around twenty minutes.

Again, I'm back to my own. I reviewed the documents I prepared in the morning. Count my money. Then rehearsed in my mind what I will do in the field. I will be going to the remote villages of that mountain, talk to the tribe people, introduce my purpose.

I made myself a coffee. My mind was already moving how it is going to be –my fieldwork, an appraisal of the communities' socio-economic status.

"Can we discuss with the tribal people? Would they understand my dialect? Will they be accommodating?" I thought. "But I had a local guide with me. She can interpret, I'll ask her to do so."

The night came. It was still raining. I slept early after taking my dinner and read some pages of a book.

Morning came. Yes, the rain subsided and the sun shone brightly.

"Oh, what a day!" I said.

After taking my breakfast, my local guide arrived with a horse.

"It's for you! We will have a long walk." She told me.

"Wow! I haven't rode a horse before, I don't know how. I just see horses in cowboy movies and cigarette commercials!" I answered.

"Well, it is your first time then! Do not worry, I will guide you how." My local guide answered.

I got my backpack and walked beside the horse. Then my local guide instructed me on riding the horse.

"Ok, I'm up. How to make this horse walk?" I asked.

"I'll pull the horse." she said smiling.

The local guide, a woman in her late-twenties did

not ride the horse. She pulled the rope and walk first in front of us. She was one of the tribe people assigned to assist in my activities.

Walking long trips was common to her.

We started our journey. We passed by villages. I saw farmers tilling their vegetable farms. I saw vast hectares of onion farms.

"Ahh, I see. This is where our onions come from." I said to her.

She just smiled.

"Horses are common here. We usually use horses in transporting our products from the farms to the town center, like those onions." She told me while walking.

We passed by shallow creeks.

"Are you OK?" I asked my guide.

"We can take a rest." She said.

We rested a while, ate some bread I brought in my pack. Then moved again.

Now, we were nearing the forest. I saw trees in both sides of the mountain. The trail was now getting narrower.

Then we approached a stiff cliff at a mountain side. The trail was only for one person to pass. At the left side of the trail was the mountain side, the right side was a cliff.

"Oh, I can't ride on the horse with this." I said to her.

I disembarked from the horse and walked on foot.

She pulled the horse. As I looked down the cliff, I saw the river below.

"What a site!" I exclaimed as I saw a waterfall that came out from the side of the mountain. "It's my first time to see that. I saw waterfalls that comes from mountain tops before. Not this one."

My local guide just smiled at me again.

After a long walk and horseback-riding, finally, we reached our first destination. We were greeted with warm smiles by the village leaders as we rested from that journey. We spent the day there. The next village will be a half day walk without the horse.

THE FOREIGN VOLUNTEERS

Upland Cagayan de Oro, 2017

"They are all looking at me!" The South American foreigner said smiling. There were two of them. The other one came from Europe.

"Yes, aside from being beautiful, you look different." I told her teasing.

She was different. She was tall, towering above the local folks, white-skinned with blonde hair. She was in her early twenties.

The local folks and their children kept looking at them. They were all smiling. Somewhat amazed.

"It is not common for them to see someone like you, foreigners, especially, at this meeting." I added.

We were at the farming village meeting center.

An old house made of stones and hard woods.

"Is this your first time to come here, in our country?" A woman farmer leader asked the South American.

"Yes!" she answered.

"How do you find our place?" the woman leader asked again.

"Cool! The people are great!" she answered again.

"Though, it's kind of hotter here compared to our place. I don't know, I got some kind of rashes." she added.

"Well, you'll get used to it." The woman leader answered.

When the meeting started, we all sat in Monobloc chairs. My colleague facilitated the meeting with the farmers. They were discussing concerns in the local dialect.

"What are they talking about?" The South American whispered to me. The European just kept silent -- observing.

"Ahh, they were discussing about the land distribution processes. He said that the documents were already submitted to the government agencies for processing." I translated to her the discussion.

"Are they going to get the land?" she asked me again.

"Hopefully. The landowner and the farmers have some kind of agreement for land sharing, after years of negotiations. We have been assisting them for some years already in this project." I said.

"Good that the landowner agreed to share the

land." She added.

"These farmers who are the actual tillers of the land for years have the right to own the land they till. Many of them have been living here for several decades already. But, this is also a unique situation compared to other land tenure issues in the country." I explained.

My colleague continued to explain to the farmers the status of the project. A farmer participant stood up and asked a question.

"What is the farmer saying?" she asked again.

"He asked how long will it take for this to be realized." I told the foreigner.

"What is he saying this time?" The South American asked again referring to my colleague replying to the farmer's question.

"He said that while we want to fast track the process, we cannot. We have to wait and have patience, since we are following the government procedures for this land project." I explained to her.

She nodded. The other kept observing the farmers.

When the meeting ended, the farmers prepared the foods.

While waiting, the European told me. "You know what? From the time we arrived until now, the farmers kept on smiling."

"Really? You noticed that." I replied.

"Yes! Though, I cannot understand your dialect, I can see in these people's faces that they are happy. Smile is a universal language, it give the same message wherever you are in the world. Happy." She said.

"Uhuh...true." I replied.

"I can sense they are happy and contented." She said.

I smiled nodding. Thinking inside that she has a very good point.

"The foods are ready!" The woman farmer leader announced.

My colleague asked one of the farmers to lead the

prayer to bless the foods.

"Ok, let's eat!" I said after the prayer.

The two foreigners got their plates and checked the foods at the table.

"What is this?" The South American asked.

"These are cooked bananas. These are cassava with coconut milk." The woman farmer told her. "We have rice and fried fish too. Do you eat rice?"

"Mmmm, OK. Yes, we have rice in our country. Well, I'll try this banana and cassava." She replied while picking the banana and cassava with her fork.

"What do you usually eat?" I asked the South American.

"I love beef. We always have beef in our place." She replied.

"Uhh, sorry, we do not have beef right now. Beef actually is expensive here." I said.

"No, no, it's fine! I am really OK with this. I can have beef tonight when we go back to the city." she answered.

"Yes, sure!" I said.

We were silent while eating our lunch with the farmers.

Some few weeks ago, these foreigners arrived in the city. They were volunteers from an international organization. They choose the country and were placed in our organization.

FROM DIFFERENT WORLDS

Surigao del Sur, 1995

"W hat is that?" the young farmer asked me as I got my bottled water from my backpack.

He was carrying two big containers and filling it with water at a spring near the forest. I was there for a community training.

"This is commonly called mineral water. I bought it at ten pesos at the city." I replied.

"What! Water in bottles! Selling water in that small plastic bottle?!" He asked again in amazement and shock. "Water is sold! In small bottles at ten pesos?!"

"Yes!?" I answered wondering why he did not knew.

I thought we came from a different world. It was his first time to see a bottled water.

"I cannot understand. Here, water is free, you can fetch water in springs, creeks and rivers!" He said.

"Yes, it is sold at ten pesos. This is good business down there." I replied again.

"Oh, these greedy capitalists! Even water that comes from nature, they are selling! In small plastic bottles?!" He now said with a bit of wonder and anger.

"Well...they find the opportunity to earn." I said.

"So, how much will these containers be? Hundreds of pesos if compared to that?" He asked again.

"Well, maybe, I do not know. They are mostly selling in these small bottles" I replied.

"Uhuh? So, what happens if you cannot afford to buy water there? What happened to the poor?" He asked again.

"I guess they have no choice but to drink water distributed through pipes from water districts." I said.

We were silent for a while. The two containers were now filled with water from the spring. Given free from nature.

He carried one of the containers. I carried the other—the smaller one.

As we walked back to the village, I said, "Know what? Now, water is bottled and sold. What if there will come a time that air will be bottled and sold too?"

"What if that time come? Maybe in the city which is already polluted. But here, it's unthinkable yet, we can still breathe fresh air. The forest gives us fresh air." he answered.

"Yeah, I hope that time will not come." I said.

After many years, water in plastic bottles became a huge business catering to millions of people worldwide. Bottled water manufacturing companies are producing billions of these bottled water yearly and generating billions of income.

However, it also becomes a problem. Used plastic bottles are seen to contribute to environmental issues, like pollution and garbage. Economically, bottled water, sold at higher cost, is said to bring huge profits only to those manufacturers –and not to the local communities in the upland who help protect the water sources.

A LESSON FROM WOMEN

Lake Mainit, 2007

T he chairs were already filled with women. Mothers carried their young children with them. The other women have not. Some were in their early twenties, others were in their late forties, and a few were in their sixties.

I was sitting in a corner inside a village training center. Watching them.

"Have everyone printed their names in the attendance sheet?" My female colleague asked the crowd.

Everybody nodded.

"Can we start?" she again asked.

"Yes, we can, it's almost ten o'clock." One of the participants replied.

The session started with a prayer. This is common here. Then, my colleague started the "getting-to-know-you" session, discussed the purpose of the activity and started the first topic.

After an hour, she finished her part of the session.

"For the next topic, let us welcome the resource person..." She introduced and called my name.

The participants clapped their hands.

"Good morning everyone! Are we all set for this topic?" I greeted them with a smile as I stood up in front.

"We will be discussing the violations against women and their corresponding penalties." I started and mounted my visual aids at the blackboard in front.

This was my first time to become a resource person for a gender advocacy and women empowerment topic. Me --a man.

The day before, I was busy preparing the visual aids for my topic. In a manila paper, I wrote using pentel pens and in big letters the major topic points. I drew some illustrations and colored it with crayons.

"How many of these violations to my wife have I done?" I jokingly asked my male colleague as I reviewed the topic guide from a training manual.

"Yeah, hahaha! Let me see that?" My male colleague replied laughing.

"Do not joke on that! Those violations are serious and many women suffered from maltreatment from their partners. That is why there is a law for those violations, to protect women." She told us seriously.

"Uhh, sorry. It is also good that we men knows about this. Actually, I am learning." I replied. Inside I felt ashamed.

"Yes. Men should know this too. The women's struggle for this law to be passed is not easy. It took decades of policy lobbying. We are thankful it is now a law. I can relate to this because I work before with battered women. I also was maltreated before by my husband." She added.

We were silent. Now, I am almost finished with the visual aids.

"So, do you think I am effective in giving this, as a man?" I asked my female colleague.

"Yes, I believe men resource persons for this topic is effective. Don't worry, I know you can do it." She replied.

"Ok, I will wear my pink shirt too." I said smiling.

"That will be cool! It will give a signal that we are not stereotyping colors –blue for men, pink for women." she replied.

The training was part of the advocacy to empower rural women to be aware of their rights and become active in their own communities, especially in participating in the decision-making. Accordingly, violence against women does not only mean physical and sexual abuses, but also, emotional, psychological and economic.

There were many cases of unreported abuses to women, especially, in rural areas, where poverty lingers high.

AFTER THE
FLOOD

Mt Kalatungan, 2014

I placed my one peso coin in the table covered with white cloth.

The rest of those around also placed their coins. We were more than twenty people around—both indigenous peoples and us coming from the lowland. We travelled early from the city to that forest village some 1,400 meters above sea level.

We were gathered around that table. Silent.

Then the *baylan*, the tribe's spiritual leader, dressed in tribal costume, started praying in his local dialect.

The ritual started while the other tribal leaders, in their tribal dresses, held the native chickens.

After few minutes, the *baylan* signaled the butchering of chickens. Then, the other tribe members helped in dressing and preparing the native chickens.

After an hour, the chickens were already cooked, placed on the table with rice.

The *baylan* again started his prayer. After a while, he signaled to everyone to pick and eat.

I took a small piece of chicken and rice. The rest also took some piece and ate.

When the ritual was finished, we all were invited for the full meal.

"This is always done here, it is part of our customs. Asking blessings from God." the tribal chieftain told me as we ate.

I nodded. I was thinking silently that for the tribe, this is a very essential activity deeply rooted in their cultural belief and tradition.

A week before that event, I had a meeting with the tribal council on the implementation of a reforestation project inside their ancestral territory. This was after weeks of series of meetings with other groups and institutions in the city. The tribal council agreed and was thankful for the reforestation project. But they suggested to conduct a ritual first before the actual implementation.

When we had finished our meals, we all went to the village hall. It was 2 o'clock in the afternoon. We were there for the reforestation orientation.

"I thank everyone for your presence. Our sincere greetings to you...and it is an honor to be working with you on this reforestation project..." I started the introduction of the project.

I explained why the need to reforest and the scheme of the project, in my local dialect.

More than two years ago, the city where I live has suffered a flashflood. Thousands of those residing near the downstream river died. The city never experienced this kind of deadly flood before. The flashflood was attributed to the deforestation in the upland caused by decades of commercial logging. Some experts said that the flood was also because of climate change –which resulted to heavier typhoons charting unusual tracks.

The upstream of the river is located within these forest villages.

"This is a cooperative effort among various stakeholders from the lowlands and those in the uplands. We need to work hand in hand in protecting the forest and managing it..." A colleague from another institution shared her message.

"Let us clearly understand that we, indigenous peoples, who live here for generations, did not cause the flood. But, we need to do our part of protecting the forests. This is where we live, this is where we get our medicines. The forest is our home, our sacred ground..." the tribal chieftain said.

After the orientation, we have a brief planning on what to do next.

The day ended positively.

That night, I slept in the tribal chieftain's house, with the rest of my companions from the city.

BEHIND THE
MALL

Cagayan de Oro City, 1994

A pack of instant noodles with a can of sardines. This was what she prepared for our meal that evening. She just came from the market selling candies and cigarettes.

"How was vending?" I asked her as we took our meal.

"Well, I have a good sale today. I earned some few pesos..." she answered. "I can buy the shoes my daughter asked for her school activity."

"That's good news!" I said.

"Yes, good thing the traffic police were not there to push us away." she said. "The other day, they were around...I had to transfer to another spot. Less people, and I have less sale."

She was a street vendor and was selling outside the market, at street sides. There were many of them like her. The traffic police were pushing them away from the street side because they were seen to cause traffic congestion.

"So, by the way, where is your husband, not yet here?" I asked her.

"Ahhh, well, I guess he is with his friends, maybe drinking." she answered.

"Ohh…umm. He works at the pier?" I again asked.

"Yes, as a laborer. He carries anything he can carry for a fee." She answered.

"Hard job ha?!" I said.

"Really. He is already complaining about back pains. He is getting old. But, what can we do, we have to earn every day, we have mouths to feed. I do not anymore complain about his drinking because I believe it's his way to enjoy his life despite hardships." she answered.

I looked at her as I sipped my noodles. Her eyes was somehow teary.

"If only we have a permanent job, like employees, we will not do this. We will not live in this place. But, we have not finished our education, because our parents cannot afford. So here we are." she continued.

"In our line of work, street vendors, sometimes we ran like thieves when police comes. Some of them destroys our stalls and products if we will not move…I sometimes think that this is unfair. Because we are just there for livelihood, and they will say it is illegal." she continued as she finished her meal.

"Yes, the government should have a program to address that issue." I answered.

I also finished my meal. She collected the dishes and put them in the sink. She kept the rest of the noodles with sardines and the rice for her husband.

"By the way, if you feel like sleeping, you can sleep here. I hope you don't mind our place. We are just poor."

She showed me my sleeping spot. It's in a corner near the dining area. A mat, a pillow and a blanket was already prepared.

"You need not worry about me. It's really fine. Actually, I am very thankful for accepting me in your home." I replied.

Earlier that day, I rode a *jeepney* twice from my house going to the city's famous mall. I stopped there. I walked passed the mall into an urban poor community just behind it.

I walked through the edge of a cemented creek side. I can smell the odor coming from the creek which already turned black and full of garbage. The creek side were full of houses made of light materials –wood, cartons, sacks, used plywood and galvanized roofs with used tires. I passed by children playing, men and women carrying vending stalls and other things.

I walked for some few minutes along that cemented creek side until I reached her house. It's a three-storey shanty, like most of the rest of the houses there. The first floor was a cage with a pig, the second floor was the receiving and dining area and the third floor was their bedroom.

Looking from the adjacent mall, this place seemed to have never existed -- hidden by large billboards and advertisement signs.

I was there for a student community immersion program.

THE UNHEARD VOICE

Lake Mainit, 2008

She was with her mother, a nine year old girl with curly hair. Her mother is attending a livelihood consultation meeting we organized for the tribal women in a lakeside village.

"Why is she not in school?" I asked the mother while we were still waiting for other participants to arrive.

"She don't feel like going today." Her mother replied.

"Why is that young girl? You are supposed to be in school today." I told the girl.

The girl did not answer. She shyly embraced her mother tightly.

"She said she is always bullied by her classmates.

They are calling her bad names… joking on her." The mother instead answered my question.

"Ahhh, bad classmates. They are not supposed to do that!" I said.

We were silent for a while when other women arrived. They signed their names in the attendance sheet.

"You know sir. We are really feeling bad. We felt like the others see us as second class citizen because of our feature –curly hair and dark skin. We felt rejected and discriminated." The mother said. She was referring to the non-tribal people.

"They call us *kongking*, among other names, which is very degrading. That is the reverse of king kong, the ape. We do not like to be called like that. In school, other children tease our children. That is why, you cannot blame us if our children do not go to school." The mother continued her story.

I just listened and kept nodding -- processing in my mind the things she shared. Some kind of pain struck my heart.

This type of indigenous people is said to belong to the oldest tribes in this country. They mostly live near that lake and the forest. They are mobile, somewhat nomadic. Before I came to this place, I've seen some of them roaming in town centers where many non-natives called them such name. They were looked down and discriminated.

"Sometimes we long for a school intended mainly for us, indigenous peoples, for our children. I hope our government can do that. Then, there will be no discrimination from non-native children." She added.

"That is a good idea. A school for indigenous peoples. I heard there are some institutions supporting that. But, let us just hope it can be done here. That will be good." I answered.

Our sharing was interrupted when my female colleague came in and asked, "Are all the participants we expected already here?"

"Ummm, the attendance is already 16, we are expecting around 18. I guess we can start in a moment. Maybe others are still coming." I said to her.

"OK, I'll facilitate the meeting, you help me in the documentation." she told me.

"Sure!" I replied.

My female colleague then started the meeting. We all stood up for a prayer led by one of the participants. Then, my colleague discussed the objective of the meeting. The meeting was to discuss with the tribal women what potential livelihood activities they wanted to pursue to support their economic activities. They were there to identify what they think is viable for them based on their community resources and their current capacity.

We were there to facilitate. My task was to assist them in packaging their ideas into a simple business plan.

THE BARRICADE
SITE

Cagayan de Oro, 2000

I t was the first day of the year. My head ached a
bit from the other night's New Year's Eve celebration and debate over Y2K hysteria.

We had debated that night over some prediction
that when year 2000 falls, all computerized ma-
chines and other computer-operated devices will
crash down and the world will fall into more chaos.

It did not happen.

Anyway, that New Year's day I had to get back to
the site. I'll get my stuff I left days earlier in that
barricade site. The next day I will be travelling to a
coastal community in another region.

Just a week earlier, I escorted a Japanese volunteer who came to the country to learn from what we

are doing. I brought her to the barricade site.

There was an advocacy concert there. A concert for the environment our group organized. Local bands played music.

"I can't understand the message but the melody is good!" The Japanese volunteer told me while swaying her hands in the air. The band played a song in the local language.

"Yes, the message is to protect the forests. Without the forests, we will be facing disasters." I told her.

"Did they compose the song?" She asked me.

"No, that was originally played by a well-known environmental band. They just rendered it." I replied.

"They play it good, huh?" I asked her.

"Yes! They play good" She said. Now, she's tapping her feet on the ground.

The site that night was filled with upland farmers, indigenous peoples and fisherfolk. Around 100 of them. There were also student and youth leaders from the local schools. They were there for the concert – a concert for the environment.

They were all in cheers. Dancing. Singing with the music. Clapping their hands. Tapping their feet.

After the band played, a fisherfolk woman leader climbed up the stage and gave a speech.

"What is she saying?" the Japanese volunteer asked me.

"She is saying that while they are living in the coastal areas, they are strongly supporting the protection of the forests because what happened to the forests affects them." I translated to her.

"And when the forests are degraded, the siltation and mud will flow to the river, will reach the coastal areas and will bury the coral reefs. The reefs are the habitat of the fishes. When coral reefs are destroyed, the fishes will be gone, they will have no fish to catch." I added.

"Ohhh, that is very true!" she said.

A farmer leader also climbed up the stage and made his speech. She looked at me with her chinky eyes wide open, eye brows raised and smiling.

"OK, OK, I'm your translator." I told her with a laugh.

"He said that all people, whether from the upland or from the coastal, must work hand in hand in protecting the remaining forests. He said that cutting of forest trees, logging, must be stopped...that we will not wait for disasters to come." I translated the message to her.

After the messages, another band came to the stage. They played rock environmental songs. The students shouted and applauded.

We sat in some corner away from the crowd.

"So, how long is this barricade already?" she asked me.

"It's been a year. The farmers and fisherfolk come up here to manage this barricade site, students too. They had schedules. The fisherfolk will come here with fishes for the food, the farmers will bring rice, root crops and vegetables." I told her.

"But you are not having concerts every day?" she asked with a grin.

"No, it's just tonight, in celebration of Christmas, a kind of break from a very serious advocacy for the past months." I answered.

"What do you do here?" she asked.

"To stop logging trucks from passing. We are also checking other vehicles who may carry illegally cut logs and timbers. Actually, we are forming a human barricade to stop the flow of logs."

"That is dangerous! Are you not afraid?" she asked again.

"Yes, this is dangerous, and we all have fears...but we have to do this. We need to. Do you know that around 30 trucks filled with round logs passed here every night? And this is happening for many years already." I said.

The rock band ended playing. This time, a colleague played a mellow environmental song. We went back near the crowd.

Eleven years after that event, Tropical Storm Washi hit the region causing flashfloods that resulted to death of thousands and damage worth billions. One of the causes of that flashfloods was attributed to forest denudation in the upland.

PART III. LEARNINGS FROM THE FIELD

RESPECT

The first and probably the most important and basic thing I learned in my twenty years of field work is respect to the communities.

Respect is very essential that it defines one's attitude towards the community people –whatever their economic status of life, culture, religion, educational attainment and political leanings.

Respect to the community -- especially to those our society defines as less fortunate --must be deeply embedded in every field worker's system.

We must not treat the communities, whether rural folks, upland villagers or urban poor, as secondary citizens. We must treat them as we want us to be treated– with respect.

One of the dangerous mistakes a field worker usually commit is treating himself or herself as above them –because he or she has higher educational attainment, a graduate of some well-known school, a professional, or an employee of a well-known organization or she or he comes from the city.

This wrong "superior" mindset transforms into his or her attitudes towards these folks. It can be transformed into words and actions that can disgruntle and offend the community folks. This is a turn-off to the community and that whatever activities that kind of field worker is trying to achieve may be a failure.

I have heard many field workers who murmured "They are already being helped upon but they are not cooperating." This is from the mindset of that field worker that he or she is the superior, that he or she brings 'good things' to them.

Also, one cannot just say "I will respect this farmer because I am supposed to." This seemed like that field worker is just forced to respect because he or she has something he or she wanted from the community.

I believe respect should not only be from the mind, it should come from the heart and from a deep understanding of the communities' situation.

It should be inculcated in the mind and heart of every field worker that these communities have greatly contributed to the development of society.

The fishing communities are toiling hard in the middle of the sea to catch fishes so we can have fish in our tables. The farming communities are the people who till the land and planted crops of whatever kinds, in the middle of the sun, so we can have food. The forest tribal communities are also the ones who manages the forest for many generations – they mold our culture and history.

We may have gained knowledge and expertise from the formal educational system, these communities have accumulated vast precious knowledge from their experiences that have not been taught to us in our school.

So, when a field worker is doing community work, one should not brag that he or she is better and superior than them.

Thus, respect is a basic tool for a good field or community work.

SINCERITY

Sincerity of our intentions is also a very important value I learned.

Every field worker who goes to the communities must have sincerity of his or her intentions.

Sincerity cannot be faked. In my many years of field experience, I observed that these community folks can easily detect whether one is sincere or not.

These folks can see it in the eyes of the person, from a person's words and actions and from his or her aura.

Believe it or not, but, the community folks are very keen in observing a person's character. Sincerity in the intentions can be observed. If they see the field worker is sincere, they will support that field worker in his or her intentions and activities. If not, they will be hesitant.

Sincerity must come from the heart, too, like respect.

Respect without sincerity of really respecting them is not good in community work. This fake attitudes towards them will not only harm the community but also the field worker more. In times of difficulties encountered by that field worker, this attitude will again come out. It will create low morale and discontentment to him or her. Then, his or her tendency to blame the communities if his or her work fails will come out.

Insincerity will sometimes result to the field worker giving false motivations and hazy promises. This is because he or she does not care of the results of that promises or motivations if it will come true or not. If these promises will not be met, it will create a bad impression to the field worker and the organization he or she belongs. This will also make the community not to trust.

A field worker must, therefore, be sincere in his or her intentions and dealings.

TRUST

Another essential ingredient for a good community work is trust –trust from the community and the field worker's trust to the community.

Trust is a result of building good relationship through community integration and confidence-building with them. Trust can be a result of the field worker's respect and sincerity in dealing with the communities.

When the field worker is in the community, the field worker should build relationship and confidence. One must learn to live among them -- eat what they are eating, sleep in places they can offer and ride what they are riding, among others. If there are opportunities that the field worker can help in their daily activities –like farming or fishing, the field worker can assist.

This is part of community integration and confidence building that builds trust. But, this should be consistent with respect and sincerity --not just because of 'showing-off'. This is building genuine human relationship with the communities.

Trust is earned.

Without trust, interventions to the communities would not be good.

In my observation, communities trust field workers who treat them with respect, sincerity and sensitivity to their situations. Even if there are two or more field workers from the same organization, the communities communicate more openly and deeply to the field worker whom they trust.

Therefore, trust is very important for a good community work.

SENSITIVITY
TO TRADITIONS

Another important virtue that comes from respect is sensitivity. Sensitivity is awareness and understanding of people's needs and condition.

A field worker must be sensitive to local traditions.

The law protecting the indigenous peoples defines sensitivity to culture as "being compatible and appropriate to the culture, beliefs, customs and traditions and indigenous systems of indigenous communities."

In my many years of working with various sectors in various communities, I encountered that each community, whether upland, farming or coastal, has their distinct local traditions and norms.

Many times I have seen rituals every time a major event is being started, particularly, in tribal communities. This is asking consent and blessings from the God and even "spirits" on the said events. This is part of the communities' culture and tradition. As field worker, one must have awareness and understanding of this.

The field worker should understand the cultural differences among communities and between his or her place. The series of activities a field worker conducts in a fishing community may not be fully successful if fixedly applied in a tribal community.

For instance, in one of the tribal communities I have engaged with, project entry does not end in courtesy calls to ask acceptance from the local government officials and leaders, the tribe will push for a ritual led by the tribe's *baylan*, the spiritual leader, before anything is started.

As a field worker in these communities, we have to respect and be sensitive to these belief, culture and traditions. We might have our own belief and ways in doing things according to our learnings that may be different to the communities' norms, but, we need to understand and consider theirs too.

Not only will we have sensitivity to their traditions but also in what we speak, like name-callings that offend them or talking things that degrade them. A field worker must do away from these things that discriminates.

It is also good to be sensitive to communities' traditional celebrations like *fiestas,* charter days, among others. The field worker should not schedule meetings or trainings that compete with these community activities. Surely, attendance is less.

Be sensitive.

Sometimes, a field worker wants the community to think and act like him or her—that he or she has lots of expectations from the community that may not conform with their local traditions. The field worker must understand their local situation.

When a field worker is new to the community that he or she is not yet familiar with the traditions, what the field worker should do is observe by doing community integration and confidence building.

In my experience, I asked for advises and guidance from the community leaders or tribal chieftains on how things should go and be done. This will also mean that you respect them and their traditions.

SENSITIVITY
TO GENDER

A field worker must also be sensitive to gender.

As field worker, one does not work with same sex alone. In a community, a field worker will encounter both men and women and people of other gender preferences. It is good to understand the societal and cultural factors and biases among and between these sexes.

In a community, if possible and local norms allow, a field worker should be aware of including both men and women and people with other gender preferences in activities, processes and decision-making.

As much as possible, a field worker should include everyone –without bias and judgement.

The field worker should understand the needs of

everyone, whenever possible.

For instance, in one of the rural villages I have worked before, there was a specific program for women and wives. Another program for the men -- the husbands. There are also particular capacity-building activities for both.

But, a field worker should be careful not to induce competition between the sexes -- instead, this is to facilitate a fair field to both –like a partnership.

Just like sensitivity to culture, a field worker should refrain from name-calling, joking and talking about sexes that degrades and discriminates one gender.

The best thing for a field worker in order to have an awareness on gender is for him or her to attend gender orientations. It is good to learn the history and struggle of women in the context of our society and the principles beneath this.

Understanding this can improve a field worker's community work.

However, basically, the key for sensitivity is treating everyone equally as human – all creations of God. Thus, one must treat everyone with respect –without prejudice and bias.

PATIENCE

P atience is a virtue, an old saying goes.
For field workers, it is indeed a very important virtue.

I remember one time I was rushing a community activity for a deadline. But, the village leader said we cannot hold the activity because their neighbor just passed away and that our activity should be moved to another week.

Pressured by a project deadline and actual situation on the field, it is annoying. But, pushing the schedule to them will not have a good result.

This needs patience.

Patience therefore is also an effect of understanding their condition, an effect of sensitivity.

As a field worker, one needs a lot of patience. What one puts in his or her calendar may not always be pushed in the communities. There could be lots of changes due to communities' activities also.

Without patience, a field worker may get frustrated and demoralized and feeling that he or she already failed in his or her works.

The best thing to do is to plan and schedule activities with the community. As field worker, it will be good not to impose his or her schedules on them. Planning with them and meeting half way will be good.

Managers or coordinators overseeing field workers must also be aware of this. A manager or coordinator must understand the community conditions and the pressures of his or her field workers. He or she should not keep pushing when the condition does not permit. He or she needs patience too.

Patience is not only applicable to schedules. This is also true with other activities. Sometimes, there is an agreed plan that the field worker expects the community to do their part – but has not. The field worker does not stop there and gives up. The field worker should understand why it happened and must continue to assist, guide or coach them.

Be patient. Do not get furious. A field worker will be appreciated more by the communities if he or she does this -- understanding their sides.

Again, to have patience, a field worker should have sincere respect and sensitivity to the condition of the people.

FLEXIBILITY

Flexibility in the part of the field worker is needed in community work.

Remember, field work is not an 8am– 5pm and Monday to Friday work. It is very different from office works that requires employees to have daily time records usually from 8am to 5pm. Then, the office employee goes out from work. The office employee do this from Monday to Friday and even half of Saturday. Then, rest on Sunday.

In the field, work is any time and any day, even Sundays.

I remember one time in a remote village, I scheduled a meeting with the village leaders. Because they are on to the farm on the day, the only time we could meet is on the evening when they all return from their farms. So, we have a meeting at seven in the evening.

Another instance, I was in a fisherfolk village, we

are going to have an assembly and we wanted everyone to attend. The fisherfolk are working in weekdays, some during the day and others in night time –fishing. Because of this, they agreed to have that assembly on a Sunday when everyone do not fish. Thus, I was with them on that Sunday.

Flexibility, therefore, is important. Sometimes, imposing our own schedules to them will just result to less participation and, worst, failed activity.

A good field worker integrates with the community. He or she build confidence and trust. In doing this, there are times that one has to discuss work and anything with the folks or the village leader during night times when they are out from their work. This build a stronger connection between the field worker and the community.

This is part of field work –and it needs flexibility on the part of the field worker.

Well, sometimes, those in the office are very keen on the daily time records of field workers that they miss to understand this situations on the field. They wanted DTRs of field workers to be filled with "8am-5pm" time.

There are situations in the field that is beyond 8-5 Monday to Friday work that good field workers do which are not recorded in DTRs but contributes to the success of a program or project.

Thus, those in the office need to understand the field worker's condition and should have the flexibility too.

Flexibility is also important in the conduct of activities, aside from schedules.

One time, a colleague prepared a very good *powerpoint* for a training presentation. I brought a projector. But when we reached the village, there was a brown out –no electricity. He could not use the prepared *powerpoint* presentation and projector.

This situation needs flexibility. Instead of using the *powerpoint* and projector, he used the blackboard and chalk. He discussed and do sketches on the board.

There are lots of these unforeseen situations on the ground that a field worker must consider and be flexible – time, culture, tradition, weather, attendance, and a lot more.

Flexibility needs patience, understanding and sensitivity of the community situation.

EMPATHY AND PASSION

E mpathy is feeling the needs and situation of others.

For a field worker, it is feeling the needs and situations of the communities -- feeling their plight, their struggles, their hardships, their pains, their happiness, their joys, their visions.

This makes a field worker passionate with community work. This will create a fire in the field worker's heart that makes him or her go and push forward -- doing without counting time and effort -- for the good of the community.

A good field worker works with passion --especially for the poor, neglected and marginalized communities.

But, one cannot have this without understanding deeply the real situation of these communities.

To have that passionate heart, the field worker should integrate with the communities. As I said earlier, a field worker must live among them. If situation permits, assist in their livelihood –like fishing or farming.

In this way, the field worker will be able to feel what they feel. A field worker will not just understand -- that these communities who labor hard to produce the nation's foods are poor and neglected -- but he or she feels it.

This is empathy and passion.

This contributes to other values a field worker must have for the community – respect, sincerity, trust, sensitivity, patience and flexibility.

GLOSSARY

Aquaculture - a method of farming fishes, crustaceans and mollusks usually in a fish pond or fish cage.

Baylan – refers to the spiritual leader of a tribe.

Capture fishing – refers to fishing method by catching fishes from its natural habitat.

Carenderia - a store that sells foods; a place where people can buy and eat foods.

Datu - a tribal leader; a tribal chieftain.

DTR - daily time record.

Elf truck – a model of a Japanese brand cargo vehicle which is smaller in built.

Fiesta - a feast; a festival in celebration of a certain saint;

Habal-habal – local term for single motorcycle used as passenger vehicle.

Jeepney – a 4-wheeled public transportation vehicle popular in the Philippines.

kph - kilometer per hour; common speed indicator of cars in the Philippines.

Lampara – a portable lamp fueled by kerosene.

Manila paper - a brownish or yellowish colored type of paper originally made from Manila hemp (abaca) through a less-refined process. It is cheaper compared to other paper types.

Nipa – scientific name *Nypa fruticans*; a type of palm considered as mangrove, thrives well in brackish water and muddy estuaries.

Powerpoint - a computer software program used in designing slides for visual presentations.

Tilapia – a freshwater fish which is one of the easiest fish species to farm using aquaculture technology. It is second to *bangus* (milkfish) as the most popular fish farmed in the Philippines.

Tropical Storm Washi - known as typhoon *Sendong* in the Philippines that hit Mindanao on December 16, 2011.

Renante Salcedo

Y2K – Year 2000.